GASP!

*A collection of musings and reflections from the
heart on the sometimes choppy voyage of life*

— HILARY JANE HUGHES —

Sacristy Press
PO Box 612, Durham, DH1 9HT

www.sacristy.co.uk

First published in 2018 by Sacristy Press, Durham

Sacristy Limited, registered in England & Wales, number 7565667

British Library Cataloguing-in-Publication Data
A catalogue record for the book is available from the British Library

ISBN 978-1-78959-006-7

About the Author

Hilary is a tutor and writer currently living in North Yorkshire. She is passionate about her faith, her family, linguistics and language in general and travel.

Over the past ten years or more, poetry and creative writing have become an increasingly active part of her life. Expressing her response to the world around her, the good and bad in herself and others, and a wealth of unanswered questions about life have helped her make a little sense of things and have been a distraction from anxiety and insomnia!

It is here she includes the piece "Without", about the waiting and longing for a child, which propelled the writing journey into being many years ago.

Increasingly, she has encouraged others to express their thoughts and faith in writing and runs a regular writing group, who have produced two collections of their work, and she has also run writing workshops.

"Sometimes writing pours out of me and I cannot get it down fast enough; other times the words come slowly but surely, and sometimes, I set myself challenges to write on topics I know little about and therefore have to research carefully. There is ALWAYS something to write about!" says Hilary. She admires a wealth of poets, from William Wordsworth to Gerard Kelly and Alice Oswald.

Communicating through the spoken word is a passion too; poems so often "come to life" when read aloud. Many of Hilary's poems or pieces, and those of her group, have been used in worship settings and some are available as audio files.

She remains an avid writer, especially of poems, and hopes that this collection will inspire, encourage and motivate its readers to respond to life, to the community around them and to God.

Acknowledgements

I want to thank God for His infinite patience, His love and creative spirit; all my family and friends—so many, near and far; "my" writing group; my minister and dear friend, Gail; all who have inspired, encouraged or even admonished me in my writing role; my faithful proofreaders and friends who have endorsed this work, especially Pam Rhodes.

Endorsements

Hilary has wonderful gifts of insight, empathy and compassion, all expressed in a way that challenges reactions, prods the conscience, feels the pain and encircles the reader with heavenly comfort.

Pam Rhodes, *journalist, presenter, writer and speaker*

Thank you for the honour and privilege of being amongst the first to read your new collection. Your writing is so vivid and expressive and truthful and honest. I have been right there in the storms and in the grip of the polar vortex; you have brought to life people and places I have never met or been to before.

Susan Walkington, *poet and worship leader*

The overriding impression I get from what I have read in this work, is the careful honesty that exposes and unwraps deep and staggeringly painful themes. There is a maturity within the material in "People" that was promised in your previous publication but which is now flourishing. There are some brutal, shocking moments which leave me breathless, but, nearly always, there is a resolution. Those that lack it, perhaps point to labours yet awaiting?

Elizabeth Ali, *poet*

What a privilege it has been to read your work! I have been transported to so many different places without moving from my chair! The poems are so evocative; I "saw" what is actually there, but also saw what is beyond—contained in the very essence of the place itself, as each poem took its shape, came into being—places still continuing to be shaped and continuing to speak to those who visit.

Sue Whalley, *worship leader and writer*

Contents

Place

Places, wild and wet and free; cities, buildings, people in their setting; seas and oceans, and the journeys which discover them, are all incredibly inspiring to me. I know I am privileged to have been able to travel and spend time with people who know the places and their cultures well.

Buda Pest

A city illuminated under intense blue skies.
Waterway and bridges, monuments and cliffs.
From Buda's heights, the panoramas unfolding
in the striking summer light, leave me stunned,
in awe of such a magical metropolis.

Roof-tiles, glossy and glinting, towers not even
close to piercing the wide stretching heavens.
The classic and sensational, the impressive and
the functional stand testament to a turbulent
and evolving history, throwing time to the sun.

The wide and curling Danube, a stage for ships
which slide past each other like ranks of sailors.
Vermilion paprika bunches, hanging like bells;
tall, elaborately decorated buildings enclose dark
hallways and secret shady courtyards behind
imposing giant doors of thick, hard wood.

Crossing the streets we sense the tram-rails
beneath our feet, the cobbles too, dust swept
against the kerbstones. Great cliffs rise opposite—
there, a woman dancing, holding up freedom's
palm leaf to the world; here harmonize the
natural and the urban in a striking combination;

past the tall white columns of Elisabeth's bridge,
another great edifice—the castle and the bastion,
the church of St Matthias and the steep railway
to ascend to it. And the river flows on past,
reflecting all upon its surface; such is the
quality of light, some colours, edges, facades
seem unreal, almost superimposed landmarks,
in this city of vigour and surprise.

2013

Budapest 2

From above the Danube, Pest and Buda complement each
other: cathedral vies with palace, pillars gaze upon the sweep of
parliament; by day, trams and buses weave, traverse and line the
busy streets and cruise boats plough the river; at night, bridges'
spans are studded with stars of lights as bars and restaurants

send tempting smells and haunting songs into the air
and vendors selling aprons, paprika and dolls, compete
for trade; monuments declare the city's glory—or its shame,
—one of these, a jumbled line of iron shoes along the riverbank.

2016

Mount Pilatus in Cloud

Lucerne, Switzerland

Moist and misty, the air hangs, mysterious,
as we swing, slow and silent at the side of
the mountain. Low cloud teases, obscures
our vision; brief glimpses of grey rock and ice
or the dark logs of an alpine lodge through
vast whiteness;

around the silver rock of the summit stone,
jet black birds sit, stark, stunning against
the lying snow, surrounded by myths of dragons.
Snowstorm: first, tiny ice crystals, scattered,
blown, then wild, frenzied flakes, flashing
before us, disconnecting our sense of
being, moving;

descending, the size and structure of the
mountain, sheer and unforgiving, melds
with a softness, an intense greenness of
spring meadows, sprinkled with purple and
yellow flower-jewels and, too, tiny crocuses,
like cake candles.

Below us, the lake, calm, serene, bordered by
steep, lush pastures, bell-collared cattle grazing.
Beside us, forests of pine and ash, beyond,
triangles of dwellings and onion-domed churches
spread across the sward.

Quiet Canal

Venice

And down a narrow alley, tall buildings rise together;
then, I stop, for I have come across another strip of water,
still and timeless, mindless of its greater brother; now captured
here between the dwellings, shining emerald in the late daylight.

Along its sides nestle small white boats covered in faded blue
sheets, pink flowers in window boxes overflow against the
crumbling walls, round leaves of sage stretching out for warmth;
ancient bricks lie exposed, close to the water's surface: some,
terracotta, flesh-coloured, cream, and others, earthy brown.

Above, peeling plaster surrounds the sills and doorways; curved,
black, wrought-iron grills fan out from the windows' highest points;
around them, the smudged grey of damp and wind-eroded walls.

And further, the kinder, pale tangerine sides of a less-weathered
building—each tall, thin window with its flame-like arch is
outlined in white—mirrored beautifully in the silent water.
They defer in turn to their pillared partners
opposite, the houses classy, porticoed, but with less charm.

In the distance, spanning the waterway, the arc of a quiet
bridge, its sides of woven iron delicate against the stone walkway.
Wandering here is pleasant, peaceful, heartening and healing.

Holes and the Approaching Storm

Bang Sa-re Thailand

Tiny triangles of air, pale blue, formed
where each palm frond is attached to
the stem of the coconut tree; some
of these flamboyant leaves bend across
their centres as they point nervously
at the caramel sand.

A breeze catches the bamboo lanterns hanging tightly to
the branches of the bale trees above; these leaves are shabby,
missing material where caterpillars have feasted.

The sea's skin breaks, now shuffling, as
it folds into the shore. Beyond the
flickering palms, idle fishing boats see-saw
in the strengthening wind and the shiny,
dark heads of local boys nod, then
disappear, then nod again into the tide.

Two dogs, strays, pad and patrol the beach,
tails high, hoping for a handout; nothing
comes; they dig, half-heartedly, then take
a dip before returning to the shade
where napping recommences.

The rhythm of the splashing waves grows louder, faster. A flash, a
distant rumble, distant landmarks vanish and the storm's about to start.

One faintest drop follows another,
falling soundlessly at first and then
the leaves rustle, the air is full of water
and rods of rain beat the ground, the
leaves, the pool, the roof; each prick
and dart becomes a hammer as it strikes.

The leaves, the dogs, the boys, the tide
bear all this with accustomed familiarity
as the storm rages on, then tires and is gone. The
beach remains, the trees, the tide, the clouds hang
around and then slink away—until another day.

Loy Kratong

Thailand's "festival of lights". A national event, it is held annually on the evening of the full moon of the 12th lunar month, usually in the first half of November. The "boat" we launched represented our commitment to helping our disabled friend, Lam.

Floating candle-flower-boat,
take our prayers and our love
as a sign of our commitment
to a girl and her future.

Others launch their carefully
crafted crowns, crouching,
ankle-deep in ocean, making
their wishes, paying respects.

As you sail into the darkness,
the candle dims, the flowers wash
away, the incense smoke disperses.

But momentum sends you forward,
the sliced banana trunk steadily bobs
on the waves under the full moon.

Letting go of the past, casting our
hopes and actions to the coming
months and years, we look upwards;

the sky is full of burning lanterns,
like a thousand rubies glowing, or
shoals of giant jellyfish, fluorescent,
graceful, floating in the night.

This evening smells of promise:
the crowds, the celebration,
the groups of people, sitting,
sharing snacks and stories;

our deed a symbol of our humanity,
yet of our faith in heaven's sovereignty,
her energy, her passion to serve the
vulnerable, to study and be free.

Bangkok Storm

In the car-clogged street, each pair
of headlamps thread like a long, long
necklace through the determined,
driving rain as the night closes in;

sudden lightning sears the darkness
with multiple flashes, deep rolls of
thunder follow; for a few minutes, one
side of the city battles for power in
the eye of the storm.

Day returns, too, for a few brief seconds
as lightning strikes and strikes again,
illuminating shapes and heights of buildings,
temples, station, graves and gardens.

Seeping and weeping, saturating, all pervading,
the drowning deluge soaks into the city skin;
a sodden urban shaking.

An enormous crack stuns, as if a thousand
tonnes of rock had tumbled out across the
streets and between the buildings.

The twinkling traffic trails below stay motionless,
then, very slowly, slide along the road as if
released, and head towards the river bridge.

Like stones, the heavy raindrops pelt the roof
and windows, rattling the panes and disturbing
our minds, emotions; we huddle, safe, warm, dry.

Under the highway we pass, tin roofs shake in
the relentless rain and bowls are placed where
holes will leak in water. But a freshly ironed shirt,
snowy white, is hanging ready for the light of day.

The thunder dies but brilliant flashes still
return and return; the rain still falls and falls,
overflowing gutters and the places least
protected from the torrent;

residents wrap themselves in plastic and hunker
down, waiting for the battle to be won, for dawn
to give them back their spaces; then, sweeping
can commence, as puddles turn to steam,
after the storm.

Himalayan Garden

Grewelthorpe, North Yorkshire

My fingers grip a wooden rail, a shady
summerhouse at my back; spreading its
skirts deep and wide before me, the
spectacle of the spilling garden fills
the senses with warmth and light;
it drips and glows as a string of sprinkled
precious stones under the forest canopy.

As the woodlands plunge, the vastness of the
garden is revealed: turbulent, intense in colours,
sizes, shapes, bushes trailing steeply to a valley
floor of grass which frames a lake: the chalky
clouds and springtime branches silently reflected.

Eruptions of tangerine and apricot and peachy
hues spangle in among azaleas' flames of cherry,
ruby and cerise and copious alpine shrubs;
corals collide with the lilac of native bluebells.

Glowing daffodils and tulips punctuate the
power and performance of the scene; a wave
of plum and purple plummets by our pathway,
between fragile ferns and glossy emerald leaves.

Such a profusion of planting and positioning, of
pattern yet of freedom; the hillscape sings a symphony
of awe with a thousand floral voices; descending beside
the acrobatic richness of this place, a hidden stream
bubbles in our ears as it dances downwards.

In the ever-changing shadow and light lie habitats and highways for
the flitting butterflies and humming bees; stone statues of birds and
metal mushrooms perch comfortably amidst the blooms and blossoms.

A palette of such subtlety and nuance, paints palest
cream, to violent, vibrant purple, the flowers at our
ankles, knees and shoulders; the form and symmetry
and structure of each species unfold with every fragile
petal, every wave of leaf. A leopard leaps towards
globe of mauve; scattered white star-flowers mark a
side-trail as it weaves towards the open ground.

The midday light and parting clouds create a
constant variation in our perception of the view.
At the lake, the breeze bends a thin and scarlet
ribbon as it floats in air above the water.

Seared through with surprise, with beauty and
with heightened interest and imagination, we
rest and watch the glistening "Samara", inspired
by winged seed's flight—tiny panes of copper and shining sandy
glass caught in the spring sun's rays; beyond, a small circle of
standing stones, large enough to lean on; hinting at their former
life—a rusted hinge or two are spied on the corners of a post.

Against the pagoda lake lie strange tubers, reeds and
wetland-loving flowers; nestled too, are giant dragonflies of steel and
glass, a centrepiece of sculptured magnolia; minute dots of tadpoles
swim in clear water where milky clouds gather on the mirrored surface.

Ascending on another path, where rhododendrons rise, our eyes are
constantly drawn upwards by the strength and tapestry of colour:
each dome of opulent delight lending harmony to the chromatic scale;
these complexions filtering the rays that beam through blooms and
branches; and still our sight is lifted, dazzled through sun-bronzed
spreading branches, leaves sparkling in the white-bright shafts of light.

We climb along the heathered sides of terraces,
an exuberance and variety of colour engaged in
charming us with fans and flourishes, arches
of flushed and blushing petals: teardrops, trumpets,
curls, bells, all rivalling for height and space,
expanding, bursting, prospering in their mountain
home and fed through leaves of olive and jade,
which, like robes and cushions, support, protect:
some, tall, spiky, others, soft, limp, lazy-looking.

On a high, grey wall, flanked by two stone cheetahs, graceful
Juliet balances high above the tumbling terrace; mesmerising
in its glory, this garden stuns yet stimulates. Liminal,
subliminal. What else can be said of such a landscape? Much,
I think, and yet it speaks and makes its music of itself.

Blast Beach Seaham

Durham Heritage Coast

Industry meets nature's innovation, as slowly,
mysteriously, this beach metamorphoses
from a shameful past. Mine waste no longer falls,
tipped over cliffs above from active ironworks,
or dumped by passing merchant ships; stains and
smudgy layers of rock are squeezed beyond the centuries;
fragments of shale and coal lie in clusters,
thin and flat or plump and round, sprinkled
in a grey-black sand.

An eerie branch and trunk of a salt-washed tree,
its natural colour swallowed by the swollen sea,
looms above the rust coloured stones, and with those years of
tipping waste, brackish lagoons and amber peaty pools greet the tide.
Strains and skeins of dripping string-like weed and algae and other
strange solidified conglomerates hold out against obliteration.

Day by day in warmth and wet, the hard crust of
history is blown and smoothed and smashed away. Weird and
wondrous salty residue filters through an almost iridescent
pasty, patchy, ochre-green, not organic but another alien
chemical compound. Waste waits for nature to erode it too,
the mines a distant memory; meanwhile it forms a shelf to
shield the cliffs from the wildness of the tides.
Far across the expanse of beach and through the
sea caves, another beach: Chemical Beach.

Sai Gon

I sigh remembering
the SAI GON river,
its breadth, its banks,
its buying and selling,
its barges, bridges;

snaking, spreading
through the city districts,
ports and shipyards;

condos rising in the chaos
between roads, beyond
the villages and ancient houses;

passageways and portals,
canals, secretive, their
muddy waters muffling
the traffic's roar in the
sleepless space.

Scene of war and strategy,
trade and tourist,
dictator of route and roadway,
lined with living:
shadows and shanties,
red roofs and white walls;

weed and pole, bucket and
palm; water plants to weave
around; strange smells
in quiet flows;

life in family, farming, fishing
hungry for a living; in commerce
and in craziness it feels its way;
a reminder of the past and
perhaps, a forgotten gateway
to the future ..?

Silent Spaces of Berlin

Holocaust Memorial & Topography of Terror

Between the stretches of solid nameless blocks at the memorial,
so stark and sad, glistening in the wetness of the morning, weave
soundless, empty pathways: rising, falling, across this concrete field;

as each gradient presents itself, my heart is torn at what I know—(still
so little), and yet what unimaginable suffering was inflicted on a race.
The "whys?" and "hows?" ring in my ears
against the steady, muffled fall of rain.

From beneath a pile of bodies, I called you;
when my tongue was so parched and I had no voice;
each time my star was spat upon;
when I held my dying mother's hand; for a million Jews and more,
that our extermination may not be the end of us.

Along old Niederkirche Strasse spans the Wall: pitted, grazed,
exposing twisted metal rods; below, the cellars of Gestapo and the SSP;
hideous plans and actions birthed where we these moments stand.
Sinister seclusion now disturbed and openly dissected.

The "undesirables", gruesomely annihilated:
through work's exhaustion,
lined up, like skittles and shot,
or hung on hooks;
left to lose their lives in agony;
held down, held back,
repressed, suppressed.

Their cries, then lost, now echo strangely over the topography of terror,
such terror, torment, planned here, in this place, on such a scale.

But away from this, even in the streets, where freedom
and tolerance link hands with art and infrastructure,
there is somehow a depth of quietude. Not silence, no,
but a kind of weighty respect. Politeness, dignity.

This city has not swallowed up its past nor has it overplayed it.
Iconic sights and sweeping architecture; signs and shapes and domes
and cranes project a confidence and
charm which tease our senses,
so that our imagination breathes in
history itself and its laden legacy.

The many silent spaces of Berlin.

2016

Downtown Toronto in February

Fine fingers of ice hang frozen as they fell,
driving us inwards, downwards; a web of
walkways confuse our numbed minds and
sense of space.

Ground level again and wind from the lake
snaps and snarls, biting my face and curbing
circulation; I look ahead—a red glove to
silence me, statue me, a white one to whisk
me onwards.

Pairs of eyes, noses, peer from padded
hoods, ringed with fur; no-one strolls,
they set their feet from east to west and
vanish in the darkness.

Wood and metal, stone on stone contrive
a thousand lines and heights and depths
to accompany my gaze.

Looking down through transparent floor
in the tower, a patterned picture of lines,
houses, streets, squares, roads are held
in isolation.

Behind the misty clouds and watery sun,
flurries of snowflakes scatter in a crazy
flamenco; skaters glide and spin on the
polished rink, shielded from the blast by
a red-bricked hall and a mosaic of glassy
mirrored panels.

Lake-shore water, air and land fringe each
other, locked too, in the grip of ice-wind.
Hopeful ducks and swans swim, pecking at
the frozen surface of the harbour-front, frilled by
chain-link fences.

My hands are dead, my thighs are stinging,
my lips are chapped and sealed, I cannot
speak a word, my face is fighting the aggression
of the cold.

Across the lake, there is another line, a mark
where water freely flows beyond a shimmering
edge of melted ice; the blurry light picks out
those places where the liquid runs, reflecting
the palest sky, tall, red chimneys far around the
bay and the descent of a small aircraft, managing
its landing on a reclaimed strip.

A flock of geese takes off and draws a tasselled train across evening's
peachy curtain; the cityscape paused in its unfolding recreation:
roads end, paths re-directed; once familiar spaces yield to a chaotic,
uncompromising management of digging, moving earth and
soaring scaffolding, preparing for invasion in the years to come.

Kylescu Song

Kylescu, Sutherland, Scotland

If the landscape sings, its song is infinitely
changing; in water, moorland, mountain
vibrate a thousand melodies and musings
from the skies, the rain-soaked slopes
and in the streaming sunlight.

Its voice soars on the eagle's glinting wings,
on the summer velvet antlers of a stag;
in the peaks and penetrations of the rockscape's
forging fingers, stretching into the watery abyss;
and on the loch—skin wrinkling, stretching
like polished silver in the off-shore breeze.
Later, strange scribblings reach across its surface.

The melody roars from falling water into
curling streams down tree-lined gullies and
in the sweet dynamic of the well-rooted
bracken, shaking on the slopes with shivering,
silky cotton-grass and short stemmed
orchids, palest pink to royal purple.

The colour, timbre, of lament or celebration
are whispers through the myrtle, the violet
stars of marjoram and yellow of the broom;
in the rolling mist and craggy contours' echoes;
soft tubes of cloud hanging loosely over rises
like a gentle ostinato to the intonation of
a choir; all these implore us to investigate,
explore this remotest of locations with its
language of the years, its compelling and
enduring character in strident chords of
strength and power; whose curtain call is
distant and whose inspiration, articulation
is a constant song of wilderness and love.

Vietnam Cameos

A relentless tide of roaring traffic,
dominated by rows and columns of
motorcycles, surging forward,
urgent yet precarious;
ladies, astride these buzzing beasts,
in tracksuits, or long wrap-skirts,
hoods and helmets,
sealed from the polluted air;

often, only a head appears
above a crazy cargo: boxes,
baby baths, huge potted plants;

a toddler, a family, squeezed
together, travelling systematically
over bridges, round corners where
buildings rise or spill out into the streets;

much honking from cars,
which wheel around the
two-wheeled traffic majority,
until all slows—a junction is approaching;

and, like giant shoals of fish, the motorcycles seem to swim
into and past each other, each finding its own direction,
without injury and with split-second timing as they
navigate their courses.

Under a wire dome,
five brown chickens
peck in vain at the dust.

In the shadow of a wall at
the side of the street, a busy
barber shaves his customer.

Across a low plastic table,
smoking chess players
challenge each other.

Above awkwardly-angled rooftops
climb some hardy pale green
leaves frothing with pink petals.

Behind a high railed gate
hang bamboo cages
where tiny birds sing.

Over the road a young woman
stoops, ironing garments spread
across the concrete floor.

Opposite, a large square of land,
partially covered, where platters of
dried fish lie: silver, orange, grey, pink.

Outside small, glass-fronted
offices, bright piles of mangoes
and bananas radiate towards us.

Overhead writhe rows and coils of cable,
haphazardly hanging close to
our heads and the traffic.

The tide has turned, small stones washing
back into the sea;
the waves still come, but do not reach my toes,
the breakers splash and retreat.

There is a pattern to these days,
though I have failed to see it.
A distant ship slides slowly beneath
the horizon;

wings stretched and hanging, a cormorant,
undeterred by squabbling seagulls,
crowns a rock;

a line of shining seaweed seems to
mark a new beginning.
A shiny-haired young woman, small in stature,
awkwardly negotiates a crumbling street corner,
baby buggy in one hand, crutch in the other.

Her new beginning.

Fell and Fall and Mill

The Howgills, North Yorkshire

Sleeping giants, the hills curve into each other, round, soft, yet
with strength and majesty, their grassy slopes belie a harsh and
stony core. These fells draw you into themselves, possess you,
compel you onward, upward, take your breath, your stamina and mind.
A path well travelled yet still, for me, an epic climb.
The sky lends lightness to the darkening
gulley and scree above, beyond.
Scraps of grazing sheep hide in the rushes below,
chestnut and charcoal ponies lean into the scrub. Heart pounding,
muscles aching, arms reaching, I stumble to a sit
upon a rough and springy mound. And white
water, like strands and skeins
of wool, falls and keeps on falling, as it has
for centuries past, yet with the recent rain, it pummels, pounds
and pours from each craggy elevation.

On our descent and at the mill, now resurrected
from its past of harnessing the flowing river;
crafts, old and new, combine to symbolize the
colours, shades and movements of the fells:

stone and metal, wood and wool and fabric, cut and
carpentered, melded, moulded, woven,
welded, sharpened, slatted, stitched
and bolted, fashioned, fastened, hung and bent and overfolded.

Like the Great Creator and yet, NO—these are but a
tiny thread teased from the GRAND DESIGN of God.
His unique tapestry of history and geology,
geography, and psychology, breathes life into our blood,
our sense of rhythm, and the seasons of ourselves.
In great cycles of timelessness—today through fell and fall
and mill, He has painted us a picture of Himself, so varied,
sometimes seeming random, yet so utterly secure.

Honfleur Blues

Honfleur, Northern France

Disgorged from our means of transportation,
the steady downpour drove us from the estuary into town.
Soon sodden, we sought shelter in a square, lined with
ugly, heavy, plastic awnings. Behind these, streams of
sheltering sightseers sat, forlorn, sipping steaming coffee
or cider from their mugs. Bedraggled waiters stood
beckoning as we wandered by, but we did not succumb.

Such a shame: the beauty of this place, its port
and pleasant outlook lay sheathed in heavy sheets of
rushing water, its southern aspect, dismally dejected
and denying us a view or glimpse of grandeur, for its
ancient alleyways and aisles just could not conceal the
poverty, disintegration, the relentlessness of rain.

We hardly spoke, for there was nothing between
raindrops to carry our voices' sound. Barely a sign
visible, we followed our feet in leaking shoes and boots.
All was rattling and splashing, a depressing deluge on the day we'd
hoped to smile with the artists of the past who had delighted in
architectural design, the bustle of the port, in ships and sails and shore.

Masts sagged with melancholy in the estuary opposite
the streets; there was such little sunlight to mark the
slate-lined frontages of harbour houses, and though
often painted in the past, they offered no idea of colour,
shape or size, as only greyness now defined them.

Saturated to the skin, we stepped in and out of puddles as
we climbed the narrow rise between the ancient buildings:
some, dilapidated, their timbers rejected, sagging as
the sea-sent showers enveloped them in tears.

But then, away from the sadness of the quay and
downcast day-trippers, a strange and unexpected form appeared
and drew our eyes upward as it fought its way through the sky's
never-ending spillage.
The bell-tower's awkward and amusing shape surged towards our
gaze; the slab of St Catherine's Cathedral slid into the space and,
solid as she'd been through ages past and present,
saved us from ourselves and from our soaking.

Once inside, the candlelight and warmth reminded us of
safety, security and the eventual ceasing of the rain.
Umbrellas shaken and left beside the ancient timbered doors, we
stepped not only back in time to saints and sandals, to the gratitude
of sailors for their catch and for their sparing in the worst of
storms, but into our own lives, their continuity and possibility.

The drabness of the day was drifting from us as we walked among
the seats and statues; arcs of light and colour lent a richness and a
royalty to each space and that which was placed within it. The heavy
rain that had weighed us and our spirits low was now transposed
to a beautiful absorption of the gift of life, our destiny and of the
thousand thousand gone before, now resting in the peace of home.

What a glorious reminder of our hope in Him, that
the present does not have to dictate the future and that
above the clouds the sun is brilliant and shining.

Dryness was eventually delivered and hot chocolate dispensed
as we determined to return one day, without the rain.

Niagara's Winter Colours

Centuries of lake and land, water and war,
convened upon this space to forge the falls,
falls so great, expansive, deep and wide
and white, savage in serenity; folds of ice,
iridescent in aquamarine, silver, turquoise,
grinding shapely grooves, its slopes, rising,
tumbling, ever downwards.

Imperceptibly, a million snowflakes strike the surface of the
ice or mingle with spray from the sheets of rushing water
and stud its veils of white with diamonds. Silent cliffs and
rocks on either side preside over the spectacle; forces create
a drum roll, frozen in time and in my remaining days.

Is this true? Am I seeing fact or fiction? Over and
over I see faces in a kind of transfiguration;
are those stars in the spray? Such a wonder seems too much; behold
where arrows flew before, where cries and whistle calls of native people
were heard, far back in time, removed from me—away, yet nearer still;
winds blow snow and sparkles on the air and distance doesn't care.

Winter colour spectrum bleeding into one wash
which swims and wipes, crashes and constantly
reforms, inviting admiration, wonder and delight.
Am I an alien in the landscape? Yet is it only here,
that sometimes I can, through a glassy staircase,
provoke a smile.

My Skye

Isle of Skye, Scotland

Serrated ridges, soaring mountains,
deeply grooved and twisted;
prehistoric scree-covered pyramids
rising from a silver sea;
stretching islands of intense slate-blue;
rocky fingers of land,
spreading, swallowed into the ocean;

tiny alpine star flowers; bedraggled,
wandering sheep;
deep glens striped with plunging white
water; the crying of
seabirds, the strength-giving sight of an
eagle, surveying his land;
caves and clearances, distances and dreams;

geology and humanity, all wrapped up in
an island of craft and graft,
of treasure and wilderness, and total inspiration . . .

People and Relationships

*Real and imaginary. All have value, all have
feelings, all have hopes . . . and fears . . .*

*Isn't this where LIFE is? All our perceptions, all our understanding
and interaction with the natural world come because someone
introduced us to them. And God—that's a whole new
relationship! So I try to say how things, events and behaviour
strike me or how I imagine they might be for someone else.*

Nelson Rolihlahla Mandela

18 July 1918 to 5 December 2013
After the Vigil

Madiba has gone.
He has gone but his
legacy and passion linger
still. In his heart and hands
were the roots of his tribe
and the discipline of learning,
observing, challenging rules
and injustice, confronting prejudice.

Setting his head and his
heart to the law, he stepped
into the struggles of blacks
against white domination; it
lead to danger, anger, frustration;
then—sabotage, which took him
to prison for half an adult lifetime.

Still there time was not wasted
—writing and speaking out and dedicating himself to justice
and freedom, equality for all, white or black, rich or poor.

The long road to his own
freedom realised after such
isolation, deprivation, he
showed only mercy and
pardon celebrating his liberty.

Then straightaway he focussed
on apartheid: dismantling it,
hour by hour, day by day,
year by year; and reconciling,
forgiving, making people feel
they belonged by speaking
up for them, listening to them,
being at their level.

And so Madiba, you command
universal respect; you leave
us the richer, the wiser, the stronger;
your fight and persistence
bought freedom, a shining example
of courage and strength; you are a
world figure, yes, but also an icon of
change, for a fairer and free-er place,
wherever we are. We turn our backs
on your words at our peril; you
challenge, inspire us to love, to respect
and to act for the rights of the poor and
neglected, the "cleansed" and those
who maybe . . . are "not quite like me."

Without

1980–1985: the worst years

Without a child, a family, without the means to get the deal that
others had (their lives completely changed
by children and run by needs
but also pressures to seem normal—yet I wanted that);
a crying baby, skin-close, a chance to love with motherly affection,
designation, but instead, my heart's despair floundered
in an ocean of depression;

the hours and days and months and even years, watching,
witnessing, enduring, battered, broken; the familiar erring
and becoming unfamiliar; bound, gagged, marooned, ignored,
records lost, misunderstood, missing, heartbreak woven
into the fabric of existence. Security slipping away.

Cruel comments and well-meant suggestions; fragile, frail and lonely,
weighed down, weary, esteem drowned—a tightening of the chest,
when, at each Sunday evening where the blessing's said, a whisper of a
plea for sanity and promise but a sigh of unfulfilment too; purposeless,
aimless, miserable company I was, and wife, I knew, so crushed.

To have lost before I'd found, to have wept for an uncertainty,
to grasp and pull around a cloak of respectability in order to
go on, in a kind of daze, half-awake, half-buried in the search
for forsaken dreams; but life could not be put on hold, so
as each dawn dawned, it was only bringing heaviness.

Coitus at four a.m. to produce a sample six hours later,
hundreds of miles away; a bed spring poking through—
it did not pierce my skin but pierced my
heart, my brain, my lungs . . . why?
I stopped asking then, dashed hopes and
false ones projected into my days,
confusion and exhaustion; where was God's plan?
no procedure, interview or plea shed any light.

Choice and freedom, responsibility and rights
all melded into one heavy pot of unshed tears; all
I ever wanted swept away, just out of reach; opening
my mouth to scream, no sound emerging—my eyes filled with a salty
bereavement, I could not grasp or understand, express in speech
or text or image. The feel of sickness, failure, emptiness and such
depth of longing; deep, deep, sad, profound, unfocused grief.

◆   ◆   ◆

Looking back from many years that followed, my joy in
mothering mixed with memories, with pain, anxiety and a
thousand moments of love and care and promise, I do not
underestimate the hurting of that time, that bitter, helpless,
hopeless time; living it was torture, not just for me;

I don't get what God was teaching me at all; but all I know is
that the right time came, at last, when grief gave way to peace
and purpose, happiness, wholeness and a recognition that
these children truly came from God and were His too.
I offered Him then and do so still, that thankfulness
of hopes realized, revealed and plans fulfilled,
of self-esteem and complete-ness, as if a link
was mended and my life began again.

Dear Older Self

Not sure how much older you are. That is, I'm ** right now, so you might be dead, or 85 or somewhere in between.

Anyway, thought I'd try and express myself in the light of all that's happened and all I've learned, whilst knowing that, unless you have dementia, (which I know is not unlikely), you'll be infinitely wiser and kinder than I am at present.

I want you to know that despite the bleak and abusive childhood, (and not just your own), you turned out OK with God's help. People say so.

You have been blessed with some wonderful relationships: your husband, long-suffering and bewildered sometimes, soulmate, who loves and admires you; your amazing kids and their respective partners, their continued interest and support which I do not take for granted; your (currently two) gorgeous grandchildren—oh dear, they're probably all grown up as you read this, maybe even with children of their own! (That makes you a GREAT grandma!) and your brother—is he still volunteering in Thailand? He says he will die there, so I hope he's still happy and needed; he's one of your greatest fans too!

You wrote some good stuff in your fifties and sixties and encouraged others to write. You had some really, really good friends who gave such guidance, comfort and emotional support. I hope you still have them, though I realise some may have passed on.

I wonder what care you need now and whether you're receiving it? Is it costly? I hope you are comfortable at least. And not lonely.

Dear Older Self: it's always easy to say "wiser after the event". Yes, you made mistakes, you worried too much, you had some tough times with lack of sleep, but with God's help and creativity you won through. So, now dear Older Self, think kindly of your younger days and enjoy the health you have, and always (and I'm sure you are) be thankful.

Love, your Younger Self

Inclusion/Exclusion

I'll pick her cos she picked me last time.
He'll get chosen cos he's Mr Popular.
They want him cos he always wins.
She'll be next, cos she's a bully.
Her as well cos she's a bully.
(You'd better be on the safe side.)
He wears good gear, she's fast.
They're strong and tough—I'd pick them.
We usually take turns, but . . . I'm
having him. Of course, she'll go,
cos she fancies that girl's brother.
He's fit. He's quick. She's smart,
she's good at EVERYTHING.

Then it's down to the dregs.
That's what we feel. Fat. Or ugly.
Spotty, awkward, lame, weird.
I don't think I am any of these things.
Clearly I am.
Fitting in.
What does that mean?
On another day, would he choose me?
No. I haven't proved myself—at sports or
anything. I'm not in the "in" crowd.
One day it would be nice if, first of all,
one of the "out" crowd got picked.
You know, just because.

Rory

Rory was a child you seldom saw.
Rory was a child who no-one knew.
Not really.
He didn't know anyone.
Either.

Rory had parents and a home.
Rory went to the school down the hill.
Sometimes.
Sometimes he didn't.
Either.

One day in summer he disappeared.
You only knew because it was on TV.
On TV.
In the kitchen.
At teatime.

Strange that day, cos everyone knew.
He'd disappeared but no-one knew
where to.
Didn't seem to matter.
Not really.

Of course a few people did speak to him,
teach him, sell him stuff, drive him home.
But.
No-one really knew.
The Rory boy.

Then, when he disappeared, vanished.
He was described as average build, height.
Blue eyes, green tie.
No outstanding features.

Where could he have gone? Any ideas?
Did he spend time on his own, outside?
Who knew?
Did anyone really care?
Seemed not.

Not much to go on, then.
How did his mum and dad react?
Ideas.
Why or How or Where
He'd gone?

Rory was a child you seldom saw.
Rory was a child who no-one knew.
Not really.
He didn't know anyone.
Either.

Or did he?

Gasp

When did you last gasp at beauty?
At yet another range of mountains more beautiful than the last?
When did fear grip you,
as you waited for the name that would make you sigh and gasp?

When were you astonished,
caught your breath at some amazing news or
the sight of someone unexpected?
When did you inhale so quickly, suddenly,
when you remembered something crazily
important that you forgot to do?

When did the numbing coldness of the water
squeeze the air from you and make you gasp involuntarily in pain?
When did your lungs struggle to exhale,
leaving your mouth open as you weighed up the
inevitable choices you had before you?

When did your words come out in gasps, in tiny utterances, because
of fright and overwhelming shock? When did you gasp with relief or
satisfaction at knowing of the safety of another, or at some surprise?

When did your past and present, future, no longer
matter for a moment, as you gasped in ecstasy and
wonder at the power of loving, being loved?

Today, as I walked beside the fence, I gasped as a squirrel's weight
pressed so briefly on my shoulder, then sprang upward to a branch!

Gasp! Did Jesus really say He loved me?!

Life begins . . . and ends . . . with a gasp.

Syrian Cry

Displaced, traumatised, exhausted, horrors heaped upon
a child, his innocence, trust, ripped away, replaced by
growing bitterness as we fail so many, night and day.

Loss and grief, despair turns to sickness, sadness, madness,
and anger, deep seated anger, sealed into minds and hearts.
"I want to go HOME." But where and what is home?
I touch . . . Nothing.

Home is where I was, my familiar surroundings,
cousins, neighbours, school and shops; places, times
of day, things that made sense. Cooking. Sleeping.
Waking. Normal. I see death. I can't sleep.

Afraid of what I don't know, I want to shout, cry out, but
there are thousands around me who are shocked enough.
What have I done? What have *I* done? Why did father
have to die? I hear shooting. If I sleep, will I wake?

I want to go home, but I know a certain peril is my fate if I return.
Yet *here* there is potential danger too, from those who would prey
on our vulnerability; forced to work in heat or cold,
or to be taken away, for my body or for money. I
smell rotting food. I'm afraid. Afraid to sleep.

Hear me, someone, hear me, please, help us, please! Get involved,
Get hurt, because you care. Infuse, entangle, understand.
I want to be safe. I want . . . to go home.
I am scared. Really scared.
I taste dust. In my sleep, I die.

Treasures and Dreams

Musings of Mary

He's sleeping now and so is Joe, but I'm awake and wondering;
I feel exhausted yes, and sore and weak and yet I'm feeling so elated, so
fulfilled and long to suckle this baby boy, who's not just mine, of course,
but will be Joe's and . . . all the world's, in time.

He'll need me and yet I know I'll need Him too; from
my own womb he came last night in this dusty old barn,
Joe by my side and the animals for company;
I sigh with tired breath but at the same time, smile—
remembering all the visitors we had . . . to see . . . my Lord!

Shepherds, lowly, came to see Him, saying this was just what the
angels had told them. Exactly. They were spellbound, humbled,
amazed and then found their voices and rushed off back to their
flocks to tell and retell the story to whoever they would meet.

There had been a song too, I was told; really grand, special,
all about the glory of God, shown here in this place in the
presence of this ordinary baby. Who happens to be my son!
I swap him to other breast and stroke his downy head.

I am aware of a power so great, so strong and yet so intimate;
a love that is unimaginable. I do not fully understand my role;
I must trust God for how to do it, for where and when;
for caring, comforting, instructing and
nurturing; yet letting go and leaving.

His perfect mouth and tiny fingers, delicate and pale among the
straw; He's mine and yet He isn't; do all mothers feel this bond,
this beautiful connection, this awesome task of loving, even in
the bleakest, loneliest times, no matter what may come?

Joe has stood beside me literally and without question,
understanding little but with intent to love me and this
child and teach him all the things that fathers do; how glad,
so very glad I am that God had put him in the plan!

Jesus, my child, murmurs now, in half-sleep, and briefly blinks;
my breast is hard and heavy as I lift him from the straw and
cradle him, then let him taste the milk, the food that will
revive and strengthen him for days and months to come.

The night air is cool and sky still black outside, studded with
many stars. The moon shines in through an opening in the wall;
the animals shift around now and again and blow sweet breath
across the shadows, but all is quiet as I survey the scene.

How long should we stay, and, when we go, will we go back to
Nazareth? I just don't know, that's why we have to trust God, as
we've tried to do, since Gabriel came. I did doubt that when
we got here to find no room in any inn or lodging house.

I feel complete and whole and valued. I turn his face towards the
breast and, as he reaches for the milk, he murmurs once more;
I take it as a sign of security, he's feeling safe and loved.

Garden

For my sister-in-law, Sue, who died in January
2016 after a short battle with cancer

A walk in the garden at night,
when a full moon sheds thin
streams of pale yellow light
to illuminate the stars, and
paints the silhouetted branches
of each season's trees,
this reminds me of you,
your familiar love and sensitivity and artistry;

A walk in the garden at dawn,
when the skies glow bright orange,
peach and crimson, when birds
have stirred and call in secret places
to their mates to look for food,
their young waiting in their nests,
this reminds me of you,
your thoughtfulness and care and hospitality;

At noon, when I walk there,
the flower petals have unfurled and
drink in the sun, their scent significant
and sweet, and a riot of colour, shape
and height decorates the garden,
this reminds me of you,
your warmth and eager appreciation of the natural world;

Early in the evening, when, as we walk,
the geese gather and fly overhead, the
flowers close, the air grows cool and the
working day is over, we sit with a cup of tea,
enjoying the space, the hour and a breeze,
this reminds me of you,
your faith and hope and timely kindness.

And a walk before sleep, when the smell
of the honeysuckle is everywhere and the
avian orchestra has flown, machines
and men grow silent, your heart beats
in rhythm with the night, and only an
owl's hoot punctuates the darkness,
this reminds me of you, your quiet dignity and sweetness.

A garden full of growing things,
of life and industry and care;
of weather, temperature and sound.
I love to walk there, even in the
smallest space, for I'm reminded of you,
and am thankful that I knew you,
for you helped me "walk in the garden",
to breathe the air of love and humility,
to sense the beauty and infinite creativity
of God;

now He lifts your head as you walk in a new garden:
fertile, majestic, surrounded by stunning blooms and
perfect pathways, just the right amount of light
and shade; no longer bound with anxiety or misery or pain;

we love to think of you in such a place:
complete and whole and free to be in God's
special garden, and ready, when we arrive,
to show us round . . .

Hexed

*Paris, 13 November 2015: gunmen and suicide bombers hit a
concert hall, a major stadium, restaurants and bars, almost
simultaneously, leaving 130 people dead and hundreds wounded.*

I am a smudged, grey cube. Stunned. Tossed between fear and
faith. Between pangs of incredulity and panes of harsh reality. One
face smeared with the ashen tears of the desolate. On another,
chipped, dull dust and desecration of unknown origin. Flat
to the floor, drab fear dreads to flicker. Edges scuffed, corners
cracked. The heavy skies sob my sorrow, unleash my fury.

Candles, carnations, washed as a million
memories. Shattered, one side of me
is scarred with grizzly torment: passionate, potent.
Yet another side of me is steely plain:
pure, forgotten, mysterious. It shares the glimpse of a hidden hope.
Like a dice, I roll, travel, fall. Another surface
lands, leaden, on the wet path,
till it's kicked. Then I rage and rattle, spinning,
thrown, across the square.

Yes, I'm exhausted by the city's sadness,
pallor, strain, and by the searing,
stretching separation from all I thought was
sane. Pick me up and clean me,
straighten and secure me. Speak to me of
calmness, surround me with a shell.
A shell of dignity, of warmth and strength
and sanctity. Restore my shape,
remember place, and find a space for me to find myself again.

I am a grey cube. Stunned. Tossed between
fear and faith. When I tumble,
let me fall in safety, help me to win with honesty, with truth,
with power, promise and with love. May I seek some tessellation with
my face of consolation. May I stand out in the
drying midday sun; mark this tragic
realisation of a city changed for ever, but a city still, though stung.

Ivy in Cellophane

Why did you keep two ivy leaves in cellophane?
Was it to remind you of a secluded spot, perhaps a rock or tree?
Or was it climbing a wall where you rested?
Was it in Spring, or in late Autumn, when its
flowers would be rich in nectar?

Such detail in its shape and size, its bottle green faded now after many
years, the veins a fragile yellow; was it to remember someone by?
Someone who'd died? Or a special someone, captured in moment?

As old as man, is the notion of preserving nature;
a leaf, as it were, suspended in time, as if to stop time and say,
"This place or this person means so much."
Ivy is a resilient plant, does this have significance?

It symbolises messages of friendship, fidelity, affection. So, did
someone give this to you? This tiny package, hidden from sight
for so long, perhaps even forgotten, with life's complicated strands
—it could be more than sixty years since it was placed there.

Now, turning it over, I think a secret may be revealed, since,
underneath sits another smaller ivy leaf, brighter than its
neighbour because the larger one had shielded it from light.
A partnership?

A promise sealed, a time of love? Who knew what would become of it?
We shall never know the source, the significance of this
souvenir, but I believe the larger leaf went on protecting
and promoting its companion until its death.

In cellophane there lie two ivy leaves, safe together.

Oh Dear . . .

I can't remember.
I can't remember how to remember.
What time is it?
Morning. The sun's in the east.
Oh good, I remembered *that*.

But no, oh dear . . . I haven't
had breakfast.
That's OK, it's morning.
Now, where's the milk?
I'm sure I put it back in the microwave.
Where *is it? Ah, here.*
What's it doing in the fridge?
It belongs in the fridge. Yes.

It's confusing. I'm worried.
I do remember, then, I forget.
What time is it?
If Donald was here, he'd know.
He knows everything, so reliable.

A cup of tea in bed *every morning.*
So reliable. Even if he wasn't at work.
And he'd smile. He had a gap in his teeth.
And he'd hand me a cup and say,
"Tea for my girl!" That's what he'd say,
yes, "Tea for my girl!"
He had . . . a yellow checked dressing gown,
reminded me of Rupert Bear.
My Donald.

Now, where's the milk? . . .
how did it get into my hand?
Oh dear, I can't remember.

Came Out!

As the rainbow arcs above the abbey
it extends a promise of God's mercy
on believers—rich, poor, black, white,
female, male, gay, straight.

Do I feel awkward? Yes, I do, because
I'm a wife and mother, not attracted
to any other—male or female.
BUT I have known and know people,
male and female, who have wrestled with
their reds and oranges, purples, blues,
rinsing them and wringing them and
hanging them out to dry. Sometimes
wishing their lives were different
and sometimes absolutely not.

Life has twists and turns for all of us.
Things happen and relationships are formed
and forged that may be healthy, unhealthy,
completing, confusing and without rules.

But can we be just whatever we want to be, or feel we want to be at
certain stages of our lives? Can I help someone be free? Be loved? Even
if I don't understand their sexuality, I can still love without boundaries,
that means I accept and learn from her and that includes her faith, too.

The trouble I make for myself or others,
the selfishness and pride I carry is no
more or less a sin that the selfishness
and pride my gay friend carries.
Must you be "fixed" to be valuable? "Healed" to be useful?
"Normal" to be acceptable?

What is Truth? God made us male and female.
He taught and showed us love.
God loves me and her the way we are.
He sees her heart and mine, our natures, too.
Yes He wants us to change, to know Him more, but He loves.
And if He does, then I must do the same.

Marriage to another, for me, is man and wife.
I'm struggling to go with any other way.
And children, and families and church, yes,
there will be hard questions
for us all to ponder. The meaning of inclusiveness and
celebration of diversity—is there a beginning and an end?

I love my kids and want them to
be happy with their kids.
They are straight and conventional.
If it was different, would I love and welcome
them anyway? Of course I would.
And what does that love mean?
Before God I still don't know, but I'd
trust Him to show me.

I will not be God. I will be and am His
daughter and so is my gay friend.
Black, white, grey and all the colours of the spectrum.
So for me the rainbow signals mercy, hope and promise. There is time.

Expecting . . .

grandson 2014

A sperm, an egg, a little life,
growing so, so slowly;
a heartbeat, hands and feet, a
head, *his* head. A living being.
Wonderful. Awesome. Special.

And so a miracle occurs,
reveals itself, as hour by hour,
a child, a tiny person swells
inside your womb, protected
now from the world outside,
yet catching a sense of what
that world might be: music,
movement, the touch of your
hand and his dad's, introducing
you to him and the love and
hope you will forever share
with him within your family.

Each tomorrow gently sees
reflexes being honed; him
squirming as you touch your belly;
then soon you feel him there,
right under your hand. He'll
close his fingers, curl his toes,
move his eyes. And all the while,
his face becomes more and more
like yours. Two ears ready to
recognise your voice.

Inside his tiny body, his organs
begin to function. And so he
grows and you do too, your
body swells to accommodate
the little life inside you.
You wait and wonder and wait some
more till he seems to fill your existence
and you are ready to welcome
your darling little son.

Mothers and Daughters

for Annabel, Chris and Pat—the "ante-natals"!

Mothers and daughters,
daughters and mothers
dependent and standing alone;

leaving and cleaving,
caring but letting her
make some mistakes
if even disgraced,
disappointed, in fear;
check misunderstanding
and false expectation,
negotiation, being clear
and consistent—ah that's
an ask when you're tired
and insular, forgetting
the gift you've been
given, to listen, to hear.

No puppetry here, but
honest encouragement,
the right sort of attention,
security, even-ness, interest;
no neglect, but respect,
letting go in compassion
and wisdom; reunion, recognition;

bearing, hurting, hoping and healing,
forgiving, devoting, rewarding, revealing,
taking, absorbing, explaining,
words carefully chosen in sympathy,
empathy, in silent assurance
and trust, but responsibly;

yearning for truthfulness even to weariness;
exposing disloyalty, heralding honesty,
pride and protection till heartbreak
and heartache; faithful but free-ing,
delivering, receiving each other from You.
The transfer of intimacy, constantly,
instantly, a release of the gift He has given,
a thankfulness beyond description.

Wise Men

Who seeks the truth, the star, the King?
Who will set their course, their life's work,
their intellect and determination?
Who will listen and proceed, pause and ponder?
Who takes risks along the way, examining
their motives and honing their gifts and skills?

Down a busy stretch of motorway, as traffic
slides past, a long-distance trucker from Latvia
switches up his radio for the last bars of some
strangely familiar music;

only for a moment, he is swiftly carried back
to childhood days and a haunting Christmas song
his grandmother used to hum. Religion matters
little to him now, but a spark of hope, of connection is
kindled in his heart for the expectation of a king.

Smoke from a power station mingles with
the hanging winter cloud as a long-legged
business woman fixes her hair in the Ladies
at the motorway services;

she emerges, checking her Blackberry
and glancing at the heavy sky. There had
been a text message. Now, she opens it
with one hand, while pointing her car key
at her BMW with the other.

A few words: LOST UR MAIL. BABY BORN
EARLY. ALL WELL. PLZ CUM & C US. KATE.
A frown transforms into a smile. Despite
her draining schedule, she replies: SO PLSD
4 U. COMIN @ W/E. X. Kicking off her heels,
she drives away, barefoot.

On a city-bound Megabus, a nervous old
gentleman tries to stretch his legs and knocks
over a handbag by his feet. Its owner hasn't
noticed but he feels bound to explain.

She doesn't mind and after a friendly conversation,
(the first he'd had in months), she slips her
earphones back in. Then, she removes one
and asks, "Shall I show you how to get to the
Tube when we arrive?" He's stunned and
overwhelmed and honoured.

Darkness is falling fast as a young man sighs
at the gate of the crematorium. Selecting a key
from a chain, he locks the gates and checks.

Before he leaves, he looks between the bars to
where the chapel is and to where that day,
he had witnessed five funerals, one of them
his cousin's.

Dust and dusk—they sound almost the same.
From the dust we are made and shall return;
at dusk we prepare to sleep till dawn and can
wake and work in the light once more.

Relationship. It marks every minute of our lives.
For every line of rails, or lane of motorway or
vapour trail, a hundred million people are headed
somewhere for something, someone.

For all these modes and multitudes there is a Kingdom, not
a terminus. A reason, responsibility, to revere, respect every
single life as if it were our own, because we are not our own.

The price was paid. A prize reward for all.
Forgiveness and a life lived for Him, with Him,
our guide, our navigator, our star. The gifts we
possess are His, for sharing and for growing.

Shall we seek the wisdom and the grace He offers?
And what shall we bring to Him—except ourselves?

Friday

"Friday is Fish and Chips! Is everybody 'appy?"
"You bet yer life we are!"
Comes the call and response, as sixty children
form a straggly circle and plod round,
chanting the well-known phrases, enthusiastically
encouraged by the formidable "Aunty Vi"!

There are stares, crazy haircuts and a stream of snot
passing from one child's hand to another as the song progresses.
Surrounded by tower blocks, the school where the club takes place
has a poor and uninspiring aspect and lacks many real signs of life.

No posters, friezes, awards charts or examples of work.
All the doors padlocked.
In the recess of one of these doors sits a rotund older
boy, trying to light a ciggy, while another smaller boy
crouches in the opposite corner, shitting himself.

This, the last day of the playscheme which a small
percentage of the estate's children had
attended, though many had quit over the weeks.
You or I might see danger, poverty, frustration,
poor social skills, extreme
behaviour, decay and a lack of inspiration.

But Vi is in her element. She's expected.
She arrives. She takes control.
Keeps encouraging the volunteers to set the boundaries.
"Let's catch 'em doing something good!" she cries.
Never enough hours in the day for her.

Coming . . .

a granddaughter 2017

Something's coming into being . . .
sometime soon. Something that is
someone, a little one, a baby girl,
all wet from birth. A new adventure
to embark on; moving forward into
a new reality; she sets you out upon
a journey which will be like no other,
the foundations of which are at the feet of God Himself.

The vessel's ready, sails set and fully crewed;
a family, brand new and soon to be in place.
We cannot charge, or dive, or pounce on
this appointment; she will emerge when
all is ready; whether night or day, the
climate and the current will align to forge her passage.

And when she's here, the voyage has
only just begun; and you will give her
this adventure, with your love, and care
and absolute commitment; you will teach
her of discovery, creativity; of the wonder
of technology and the wonders of the natural world.

She will learn the times and tides of men,
(and women!) about encouragement and
the dignity of all. She'll be yours, and yet
her own; her character, uniquely blending
some of each of yours, but also her own
splendid, different ways of acting, doing things
and making an adventure of her own.

Baby Love

Baby, baby,
I look at you now,
so peaceful, so perfect;
you trust entirely in me,
and that's an awesome task.

Sometimes I'll let you down—
(I'll try not to, but I know it will happen).
Sometimes you'll let me down,
I know, we're frail humanity.

But baby, baby,
I love you now with a heart
that's bursting; I love you
emotionally, but also practically;
I nourish you, cherish you,
protect you, unconditionally.

It's hard work, I don't mind saying—
YOU don't know it's the middle of the night and
you've woken me from a brief slumber, but I do!

But baby, baby, I'll do my best, and,
when my best is tested,
I still intend to love you
with every fibre of my being.

What a gift you are, dear baby!
Looking at you, all calm, so sweet,
I trust the Father to enable me to love.

Nature and Muse

*Here, the pieces are less places, more timeless spaces
and opportunities; questions, reflections . . .*

Hilltop Grasses

Some stand tall, straight, confident,
many lean in or over each other,
some coerce, cajole, caress,
others listen, turn and wave
and then they in turn are mingling
with the new ones growing there
and shape and shower each other with
grace and form and attitude.

Picking Blackberries

Proud, black and shiny jewels, gleaming
amongst the thorns and nettles; pick the
plump ones, leave the small tight-lipped
green or pinkish ones; reach for the orb
hiding under a leaf, or a bright array of
five fruits on their drooping branch; some,
selected, break, dissolve; others, firm, ripe,
perfect for eating in a moment, a subtle
blend of sharp and sweetness; store the
rest for secreting in a pie; leave some to
mature, sustain their berry life, then ripen,
others to die or be plucked by the birds
(who must be full already!); there's more
to flourish, more to harvest; be patient,
for this bumper crop each day has more
to reveal, to yield to my grasp and stain
my fingers in a rich red burgundy.

Flying West

Thousands of feet above the Eastern world,
wave ripples tap at wooded islands, balls of
cloud compete for height; a thousand tributaries
and estuaries surround the coast of Myanmar.

Flooded fields and roadways and the slim arcs
of bridges over brown rivers span my view and
then . . . into the cloud . . . and out again to yet
more water, snaking its way across the landscape
in every direction.

Now we cross the Bay of Bengal's turquoise seas
and over those mountain ranges, deserts and
wilderness not shaped by man or machine,
but only by the weather and the changing climate;
striped and grooved peaks and folding valleys,
their vast domain only truly revealed in flight . . .

. . . and further on, we glimpse below, the mountains of
the Caucasus, bluish-white, before the dark returns and
only minute pricks of light dictate a human presence.

Lord, this is such a diverse world, rising land
and windswept plains, shrunk within the watery
volume of the rivers and the oceans; we know
and communicate so quickly and so much, and
yet there are great seas of activity and landscape
we cannot understand, perhaps we never will.

For this opportunity to soar over a small part of
the planet You made and gave us, I'm so thankful.
May I welcome the revelation of the minuteness
of my mind and the awesomeness of You and
all You have created; may I work for peace, for hope
and understanding, wherever I may find myself.

The Reign Of Polar Vortex

Sweeping, slicing through the days and
darkness; valleys, mountains, prairies, towns,
this swirling, arctic Queen of ice only has to
point her finger to transform a landscape,
lakescape, seascape—who can tell her spell?
Severe she is, as she scans and scours her
foe; strong and extreme, determined and
deliberate; lifting fields, pathways, rivers,
into mounds and curls and unknown shapes.

Forests, frore and feathered: trunks and
branches leaning with hanging bluish teeth;
flora, fauna, algid with the bruma-bite of her
violent vortex; frost and snow, snow and frost,

freezing rain, blizzards thrash about as she
pushes on, pursuing her path of punishment
and persistent pain with icy pellets; in her
wake, her frosted skirt-frills have scythed
the land, trees, buildings, and left a heavy,
strange and gelid, monochromic scene.

After her prevailing and prolonged screams,
the wailing winter monarch then casts a
deadly silence. In cities, streets are lined
with ice-locked cars and trucks; brave beings,
numb in mind and body, woolly-wrapped and
booted, shuffle, slide across their vague and
baffling surroundings, searching for the familiar,
a friendly, former route, trapped here in an
unprecedented winter wilderness.

And by the lake, the chains that line the dock
today wear long and glassy fangs which weigh
them down. Boats, once glossy, glamorous,
are weak and wonderless, still, under the snow.
The soil beneath, soaked and solid, frozen, frigid,
is swelling, expanding, till, suddenly, it has nowhere
to go and so, it snaps and splits to make a jagged
crack, exploding, with a boom that echoes in the
valley, bouncing from the lake—a frost-quake.

Housebound, looking out, even the tramps
have found a room to hide in, a shelter from
a certain death; and a prisoner on the run is
no match for the Polar vortex, returning
to the surety and safety of jail—no hardship
now, compared to this! We cannot fight, our
state is frozen till the thaw, and so we linger
over latte, conjure casserole and cookies
and get used to waiting, winter-waiting . . .

Freedom

A baby knows such freedom,
yet she does not understand it;
she cries, she smiles, she waves;

she jumps and squeals, according
to her needs: to temperature
or taste or sound or sight.

Focusing, her face lights up,
or frowns at simple things.
She has no judgement,
no awkwardness or duty;
she speaks and we all listen;
she reaches out for something
she desires to encounter.

She has few insecurities for
she's never been rejected;
she's no-one to impress, manipulate
or take revenge upon.
She expresses what she thinks or
feels, without a moment's hesitation.

She delights in her own-ness,
in her expanding world, in her
abilities and opportunities.
Reacting to sudden, unexpected sounds
or unfamiliar faces, she cannot reason
or discern what is good or bad, or safe.

She relies completely on her mother,
and her father and those she knows so well;
she gives them all the love they show
to her and more, because she's new
and beautiful and life is real, there's
no tomorrow, just each moment of the day.

Almost all my observations point to an
intensity of love and of embrace:
an embrace of life, of love and of oneself;
as sure as she can be of being cared for,
loved and valued, she is unique, as I am,
we are, too.

A baby teaches me such freedom,
yet too often I forget this way of life;
I thank God for this innocence and trust;
I must quit my criticism—the way I
penalise myself and others; I must
reach out and grasp; reach out and love,
own the freedom that I have, and thank Him.

Eclipse

March 2015

Breakfast over.
But birds are back in the branches.
Grey streaks across the morning sky.
Sun seems to be proudly pushing through.
Smoky, swirling clouds.
Morning shifts to twilight.
Shadows drift and dream.
It's a little chilly now.
Is a dragon stealing light?
Two discs slide in the centre of the cloud.
A quiet, reverent darkness.
Steadily, the shadow moves.
The sun with a wide smile,
the darkness slinks away,
almost apologetically.
We are standing on a planet
watching the moon's mock mastery.
Returning rays punctuate the morning.
Sun's surface is restored.
Birds fly again. A car hums down the road.
Eclipse over. The sun has not been
swallowed. He serves us well again.

Winterscape

Behind the shivering leafless trees,
float thin, creamy clouds, eastwards,
on a sea of palest blue. Winter sun
streams across the harsh fields, pasty,
bare of crop or beast; shadows fall
beside a rapid stream. Before the
gently swirling cloudscape soars the
forked-tailed silhouette of a Red Kite,
who often hunts here; a lethargic cat
slopes beside a wall, viewing his
territory from this boundary. Fringes
of ivy flap, like skirts, from around the
tree trunks; stiff bushes, shaking in the
chilly air, stare from shining puddles.
Mist and damp cling to the land, hiding
mystery and delight, snowgrains, suspended.

Rose Wild

Beside and around us in the pathways
by the meadow, bloom graceful, rambling
roses, so soft in hue; yet this fragrant
fountain of summer is strong, wild,
scrambling over itself, or hedge or gate
or fence with small, hooked spikes,
gripping and grasping as it grows upwards,
outwards, and as it climbs, opens its
pale flowers to the strengthening sun.

From each stalk's rim cling five fragile
petals; each flower's delicate shade subtlety
varied from its neighbour's—some of light
champagne, others fainter, almost white;
at its centre a cluster of butter-yellow
stamens, crowned with orange, protected
in the rose flower's gentle glove. And so
deep greenness of leaves and grassland
is sprinkled with brilliance of rose blooms.

Night Sea

Night-sea, slate-black, grazes its own
skin as it signs itself in—fluorescent
chalk-white scribbles fan, then fizzle
out beneath us on the hidden shore.

As lights dim, shore sounds stop, air cools
and freezes, the tide turns but no-one sees
it; signatures grow faint and distant, and
a secret sea hangs only in our imagination;

till clouds filter the early light of dawn;
slate-black melds into silver-grey, the
horizon's scratched into a pallid sky and
day-sea's skin pulses with promise.

Making a Living

Where a multitude of stripy scarves surround
and clothe an aged ficus tree, tuk-tuk drivers line
the street; nylon-gowned stall-holders proffer
trays of steaming noodles and coolie-hatted
women brush debris sideways against the
high kerb; the scent of jasmine garlands hangs in
the air and a rose-frocked masseuse beckons with a
white-toothed smile and a cup of ginger tea.

Under sky and twisted cables, my parasol
does not deter relentless heat; I change direction
down an alley, part in shade. It's grey, but for a
flurry of spreading leaves flaunting their green
from frilly-edged pots. To one side, collected,
organised: tyres, brake drums, rods and shafts,
partly clothed in sheets of corrugated iron;
a strange beauty; a wardrobe for vehicles.

Mixed Motives

(don't we all have them?)

an amalgam of tradition *rejection* perception
reasons *inadequacies* **compassion** *impurity*
a fusion of *approval* **assertion** *validation*
endorsement *recognition* **care** *control*
a brew of **concern** involvement *reputation*
sympathy *autonomy* **identification** *taintedness*
a merging of *security* flexibility **sharing**
alignment of story *promoting* revealing
a jumble of persistence **empathy** opportunity
a mosaic of **doing great work** *fear of failure*
health energy *pain* hunger *mood* change
a confection of freedom destiny *pursuit*
leaving a personal legacy **responsibility** *weakness* a blending
and a striving to **make sense** of where the **thing that makes me
feel alive** aligns **with the big-picture** happiness *manipulation*
a **searching** for places where **passions and strengths** can
impact the world **making a difference** *selfishness*
the chance to **improve** society in a meaningful way
family time quality time **providing value** *attention*
accomplishment **enhancing lives** all these
soak in and become the blood, the movement
and the voice of mixed motives—I can only
offer them all to God who made me and accepts me
motivated, demotivated, mixed . . .

Essentially

In life, what is essential?
This question may have
different answers as we age
or as our health or circumstances change.
Essentially.

In reality there are very few "essentials"
as most can easily be obtained
where we are going if we forget
to pack them. Perhaps our "essentials"
point to insecurities rather than
to real requirements.
Essentially.

But what of Life? What of those
times of challenge or of fear?
Where then can we find
fundamental strength, or help,
or a map to see our way,
to clear our heads, to know
we're safe and loved and have
a purpose and a home?
Essentially.

Then shall we find we've packed
the absolute necessities of life—
the fundamental starting blocks
and then the nourishment
we need to win the race?
Essentially.

The character whose *essence*
we'll display of course, is Him,
how foolish not to see it!
Those oils that are called "essential"
contain the very fragrance of
the plant from which they come.
Essentially.

We shall find that indispensable
wisdom, that key to wholeness and
effective ministry and care when
we read His word, when we sing
and praise and listen to Him;
when we are accountable through
faith and through our trusted friends.
We must make room for these.
Essentially.

Crying

I feel like crying.
A mixture of tiredness
and anxiety, responsibility
and unresolved strands
of future plans divide
and separate me from
the world I'm in.
The past and the ugliness
I perceive in me in
tension with what I
know I am in Christ.
These thoughts niggle
and nag and they define
me, become me. And,
then, I feel like crying.
Again.

I like to laugh. Anticipate
the tears that flow with
unrestrained joy and
amusement. In a moment
a plain, dull, ordinary thing
becomes alight with colour,
sound and bubbles of emotion,
needing to be released.
Just then, nothing else matters
but the funny thing—the
thought, the action or the
notion that sparked the laughter,
so powerful, so embracing,
so engaging, they release
the child in me.

Sleep. Oh amazing, deeply
satisfying sleep. I like to sleep,
to rest, to dream, to be in
another world sometimes,
it seems as real as waking.
Deprived, I drag myself around,
close to the ground, looking down.
I feel like crying, cannot, but I
feel it. Fulfilled, I'm calm and
chilled. I lift my head, I seek,
I look beyond myself, it's more
like laughing, really. Don't
stop to analyse, just realize,
and Life comes running.

Cold Call

(from a call centre)

Indistinct background noise, talking, humming,
machinery. A gentle voice cuts through, (but laughter
in the next booth). "Hello, is that Mrs Broome?"
"Who's speaking?" I reply.
Dead.

Again, a ring: pick up, laughter.
The connection made, a heavily accented voice launches his campaign
about—a boiler, my computer, a prize I may have won.
An "accident" I had, unpaid PPIs, a home improvement scheme,
a problem with my internet, my phone, my personal details.
MY PERSONAL DETAILS?!

"Wait! Stop!"
Politely I decline to speak, or even acknowledge who I am.
"Good morning to you," I declare and hang up.

Within moments, he is back, "Madam, I had
not finished my call with you!"
"But I have!" I think, and ask him not to call again.

And then, VERY SOON, the phone rings.
This time I pick up but do not answer.
The same crackling noise is there,
a background of many voices, each with their own conversation.
"Madam, are you there? Please listen to me—my name is
Rajiv . . ." "Well, Rajiv, you are on a loser here." (I think).
"Rajiv, I don't know why you're doing this job.
Maybe this is the best you can find wherever you are living.
However, I will not talk to you today, or any day;
you are invading my privacy. Do NOT call again."

How often this occurs.
How often it is hard to understand the caller on the other end;
the lines are poor, the workers, strongly accented,
outsourced and unrelated
to the companies they are calling on behalf of.

I will not be persuaded or invited by an unknown source. Even though
the caller is not to blame. The call centre abroad may cut costs, but
now fires back at the companies who base their callers overseas.

Dear Rajiv,
I hope you don't mind, but I hope your "victims"
are not persuaded to listen to you today.
I hope you begin to realize this is a dead-end job.
I hope you begin to think of us as real people.
I hope you'll use your skills in a different way and
still have money to put on your family's table.
Targets, eh?

Lights Off in the Mind

"Everything happens for a reason"—really? Or is life a series of
random events? Our age and stage of life, our pathway and our
upbringing, our success and our failures, relationships of now
and yesteryear, all combine to shape and charge our minds.

Those we love, (and those we don't so much),
those who care for us and we for them,
those who dictate our lives and how we
lead them (from office blocks in distant cities);
our hopes and dreams and dearest longings,
our fears, anxieties and mistakes, all are buzzers,
flashlights which haunt us in the night, awake or asleep.

They distort our field and frequency, they surge;
there is no switch to close their circuit, they
impede our rest and relaxation; convey messages
of negativity, of obsessive unrealistic outcomes,
of self-admonishment, of cowardice and shame.

Lord, I've tried to ask You in the tangle of these moments,
please step inside, please step right inside my brain,
and infuse it with Your Love, Your peace, Your power
to eliminate these awful terrors of the night.
I ask again, "Please release their charge from me
and stay and keep me in your arms where I know no
evil will entrap me, as I spend my nights."

Until Today

a unique day, even as it looks like yesterday;
there is no borrowing, remembering;
the midday sky is a plunge pool,
the street and houses have an honest shine;

above the river, a parent branch extends,
affording life to its thousand children;
its heart is wholeness and compassion,
it composes confidence and calm;

there is no need for familiarity, the
page is blank and has no watermarks,
no best sellers, no updating,
welcome writes itself into the fingers;

it's like a promise has been kept
with no remembering, and possibility
has been exchanged for certainty;
now is the content of summer—

it's shouting in its freedom, convincing in
its hope, extending every stem and vein
into the sunlight, crediting itself with laughter
and completely centring the soul.

Printed in Great Britain
by Amazon

52748399R00056